JUN - 9 2017

Spotlight on Kids Can Code

Understanding Coding Using CONDITIONALS

Patricia Harris

PowerKiDS press.
New York

Published in 2017 by The Rosen Publishing Group, Inc.
29 East 21st Street, New York, NY 10010

Copyright © 2017 by The Rosen Publishing Group, Inc.

All rights reserved. No part of this book may be reproduced in any form without permission in writing from the publisher, except by a reviewer.

First Edition

Editor: Greg Roza
Book Design: Michael J. Flynn

Photo Credits: Cover Stephen Simpson/The Image Bank/Getty Images; cover, pp. 1, 3–24 (coding background) Lukas Rs/Shutterstock.com; p. 5 Frank Fennema/Shutterstock.com; p. 7 https://commons.wikimedia.org/wiki/File:John_McCarthy_Stanford.jpg; p. 9 (girl) Monkey Business Images/Shutterstock.com; p. 9 (cloud) kontur-vid/Shutterstock.com; p. 9 (ice cream) stockcreations/Shutterstock.com; p. 13 wavebreakmedia/Shutterstock.com; pp. 14–15 Marian Weyo/Shutterstock.com; p. 19 Africa Studio/Shutterstock.com; p. 21 (cat and dog) Susan Schmitz/Shutterstock.com; p. 21 (frog) kazoka/Shutterstock.com; p. 21 (crow) Ana Gram/Shutterstock.com; p. 21 (eagle) Serjio74/Shutterstock.com.

Cataloging-in-Publication Data

Names: Harris, Patricia.
Title: Understanding coding using conditionals / Patricia Harris.
Description: New York : PowerKids Press, 2017. | Series: Kids can code | Includes index.
Identifiers: ISBN 9781499428070 (pbk.) | ISBN 9781499428261 (library bound) | ISBN 9781499428858 (6 pack)
Subjects: LCSH: Computer programming–Juvenile literature. | Programming languages (Electronic computers)–Juvenile literature. | Computers–Juvenile literature.
Classification: LCC QA76.52 H37 2017 | DDC 005–dc23

Manufactured in the United States of America

CPSIA Compliance Information: Batch #BW17PK: For Further Information contact Rosen Publishing, New York, New York at 1-800-237-9932

Contents

What Are Conditionals?....4
Formalism....6
Understanding Conditionals....8
If-Then....10
If-Then-Else....12
Else If....14
Loops....16
Lists and Tables....18
Your Turn to Try!....20
Conditionals Are Important....22
Glossary....23
Index....24
Websites....24

What Are Conditionals?

Conditionals are **statements** that are either true or false depending on the situation. In coding, conditional statements represent an "if-then" situation. That means if something happens, then something else will happen.

A conditional in real life may be a situation in which you must make one choice. Conditionals can also be situations in which you must make a choice over and over again.

To understand one-choice conditionals, think about Robert Frost's poem "The Road Not Taken." This poem is about two paths that **diverge** in the woods. The speaker takes the one less traveled. The speaker tells us that doing this made a big difference in the outcome of his life. To understand repeating a choice, imagine walking a dog around your neighborhood and choosing to take the same path every day.

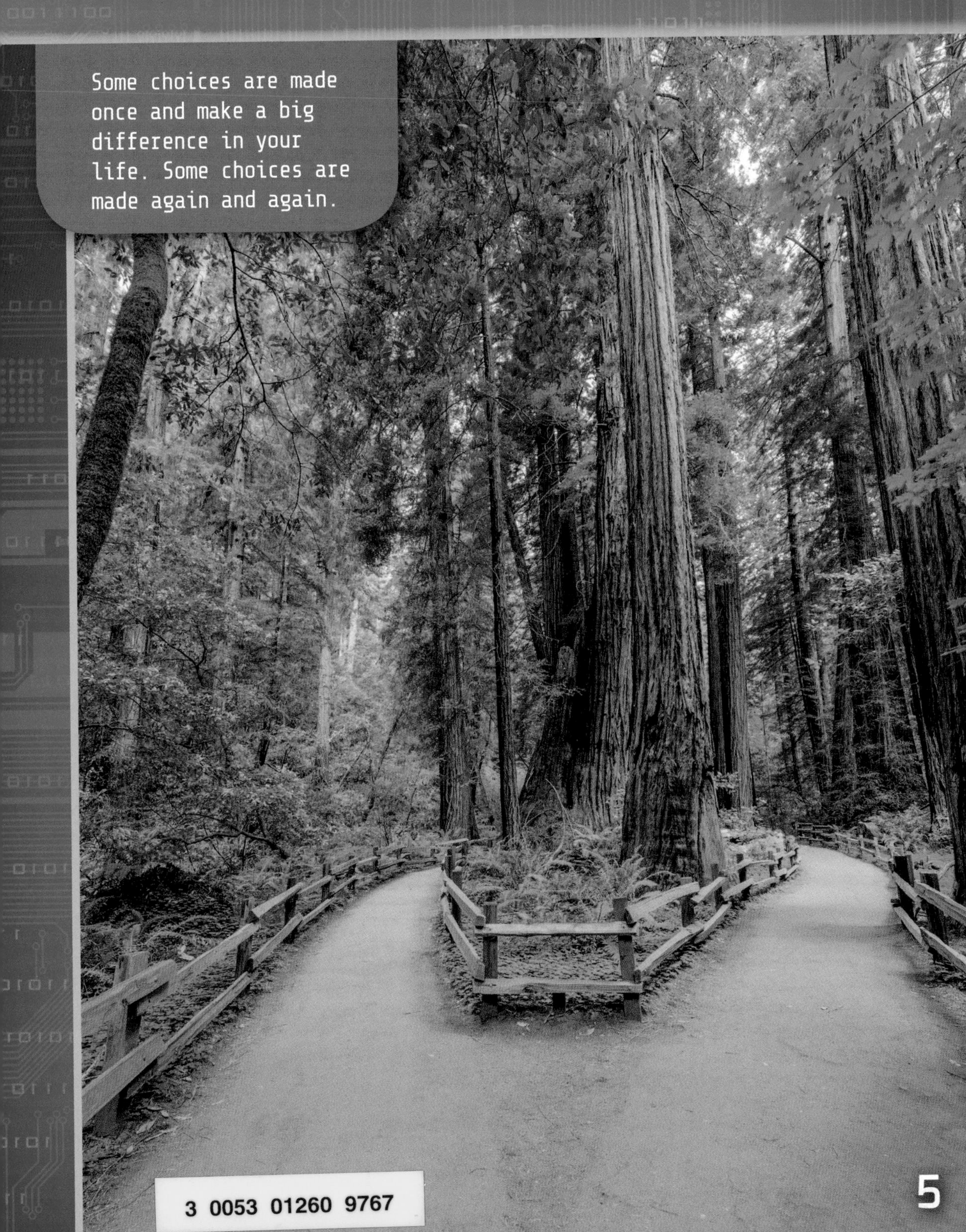

Some choices are made once and make a big difference in your life. Some choices are made again and again.

3 0053 01260 9767

Formalism

John McCarthy was a computer scientist and mathematician who worked in **artificial intelligence**. He helped create two **computer languages** and introduced the concept of **time-sharing**. Time-sharing was popular in the 1960s and 1970s.

In 1963, McCarthy introduced a theory that became known as McCarthy formalism, which states the importance of recursion. Recursion in computer science means that the solution to a problem depends on the solution of smaller parts of the same problem. McCarthy's theory helped computer programmers better understand conditional statements in code.

It's not surprising that with all his work in computing and mathematics, McCarthy wanted to address the idea of conditionals in programming. He applied his knowledge of **logic** and programming to **clarify** concepts that are used today in coding.

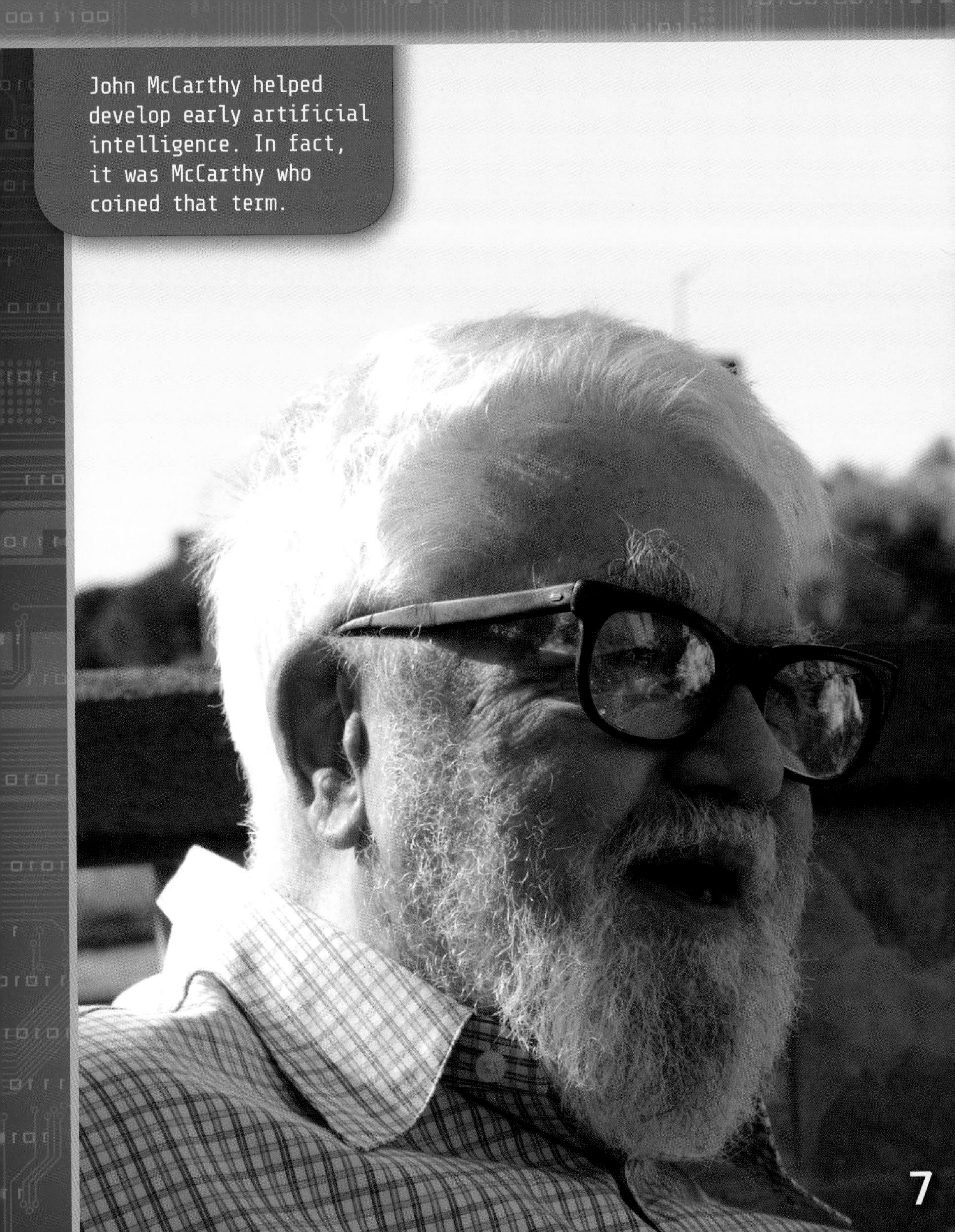

John McCarthy helped develop early artificial intelligence. In fact, it was McCarthy who coined that term.

Understanding Conditionals

Conditionals in real life don't always produce the result you're expecting. Imagine your parent tells you, "If you eat your vegetables, then you will get dessert." This is an "if-then" conditional statement. However, what if your parent has forgotten to buy dessert? What if it's time for soccer practice and you get home just in time for bed? In that case, you'd get no dessert! Therefore, the conditional was not completed correctly.

Since computers can't lie, well-created conditionals in coding always work the way you plan for them to work. Conditionals in computer languages can often be even easier to understand than conditionals in English. There are a few popular computer languages to choose from, such as Ruby, Python, and Java.

"If-then" statements imply that if a certain condition applies to a situation, then a certain outcome will happen.

If-Then

Computers work with the information they're given. They can't add additional requirements for conditionals to work. Your parent, on the other hand, can leave out important information and give it to you after you've eaten your vegetables. For example, when you finish your vegetables, your parent might say, "No dessert until you've done your homework." They added an additional requirement for earning dessert. Your parent is surely not a computer!

"If-then" is an important statement in coding as well as in life. The statement may look a little different in different programming languages, but the behavior is the same. As you will notice in the examples on page 11, regular code doesn't look like pseudocode. The code examples don't include the words "if" and "then." However, they do signal "if" and "then" with other characters.

Breaking the Code

Boolean logic is the logic that computer programs use to determine if a statement is true or false. This system works well with computers because computers only work with values of one and zero. One means true and zero means false.

pseudocode for "if then" statements

If (Boolean condition)
Then (consequence)
End If

Pseudocode is intended for people to read, not machines. It's often used to explain code in books and articles. It's also used in computer program development before the code is actually created.

Python programming language

```
age=8
if age > 7 :
    print ("age is ok")

```

Ruby programming language

```
my_age = 10
if my_age > 8
     puts "I'm a great age!"
end

```

If-Then-Else

"If-then-else" is an important **variation** of the "if-then" statement. In the "if-then" statement, the program moves to the next line of code if the "if" statement is false. Including an "else" statement means that the program will follow that direction before moving on to the next step in code. Below, you can see the pseudocode for "if-then-else."

Can you think of an "if-then-else" statement in real life? If you clean your room, then you will earn five dollars—or else you will pay five dollars because someone else will clean your room. With an "if-then" conditional, you simply wouldn't receive money for not doing chores. However, when you add the "else" part, there is a clear consequence for not cleaning your room: someone else gets paid to do it.

pseudocode for "if-then-else" statements

```
If (Boolean condition)
   Then (consequence)
   Else (alternative)
End If
```

Ruby programming language

```
my_age = 11
if my_age == 10
     puts "Your age is 10."
else
     puts "Your age is other than 10."
end
```

Look closely at the Ruby programming language example. The **output** will be "Your age is other than 10." If you change the first line to "my_age = 10," the output will be "Your age is 10."

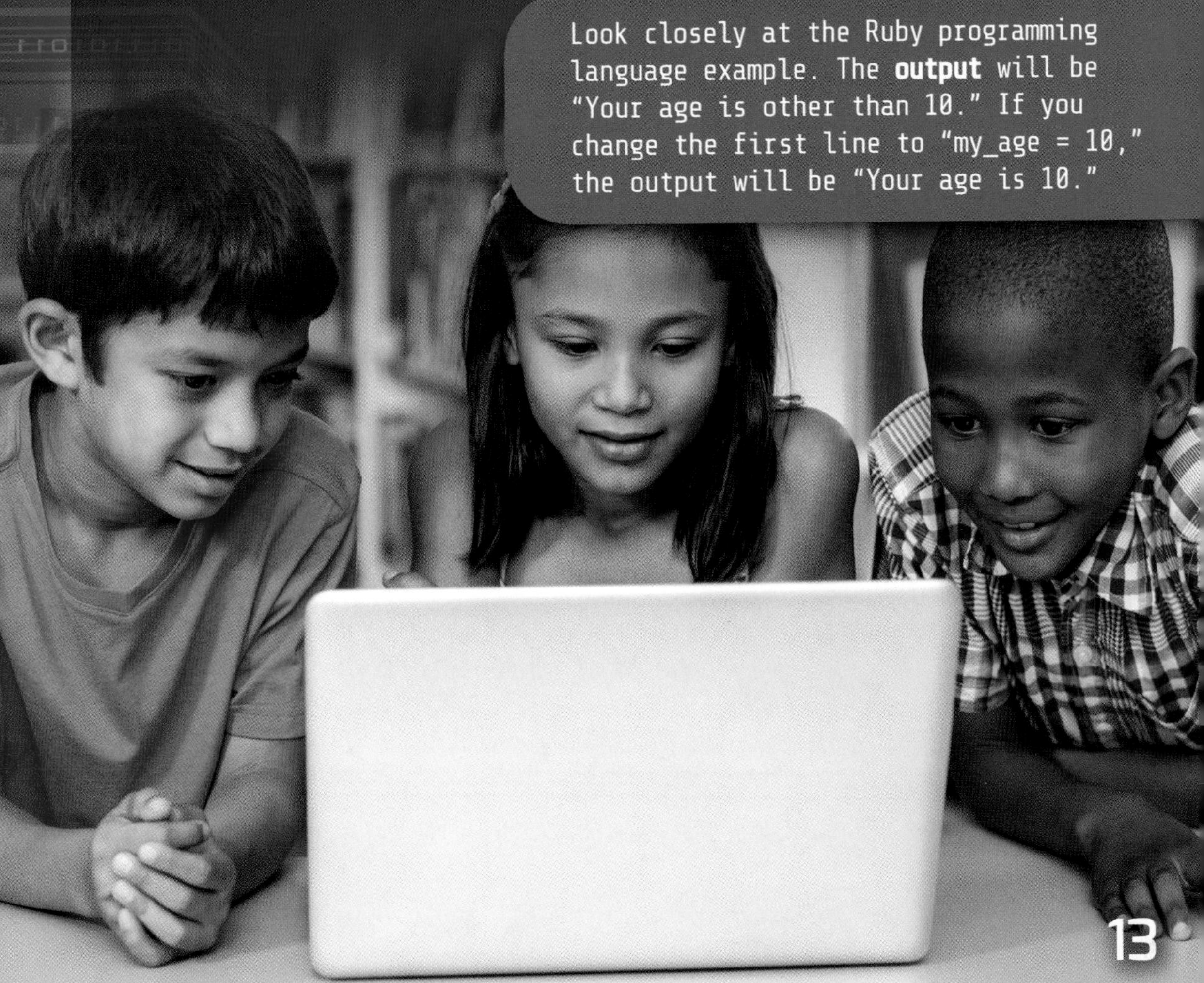

Else If

"Else if" is a conditional statement that allows you to test several conditions. That means that several "else" statements can follow one "if" statement. The first statement found to be true would be executed, or carried out. All other statements would be skipped, even if they are true. In Python, the word "elif" is used for "else if." In Ruby, the word is "elsif."

The output of the program on page 15 is "You are over 10!" If you change the first line to "my_age = 10," the output is "Your age is right." If you change your age to "8," the output is "You are younger than 10!" Instead of coding "my_age" as a set number, you can ask friends to enter their ages and test the program's response.

```
my_age = 11
if my_age == 9
     puts "You are a great age!"
elsif my_age == 10
     puts "Your age is right."
elsif my_age > 10
     puts "You are over 10!"
else
     puts "You are younger than 10!"
end
```

"Else if" can take many forms in computer programming languages. This is an "elsif" statement created in Ruby.

Loops

Loops control how many times a set of code will run in a program. Loops operate much like repeating "if" statements. Some languages have loops that are set to run a given number of times.

Here is a picture of an example loop in coding for the program LEGO WeDo™. As in all loops, the code to be repeated will be grouped in some way. The loop also includes an instruction for when the code should stop.

This WeDo code tells a motor to turn 50 times and then a horn sounds 11 times. The loop causes these actions to repeat three times.

Python uses a loop similar to the one in WeDo. It's a "for" loop. The "for" loop runs for the specified time. In the code below, the "x" is just a name for the **variable**. This code prints the word "Hello" three times:

```
For x in range (0,3):
    print "Hello"
```

Both "for" loops and "while" loops are used when actions need to be repeated.

"While" loops repeat an action as long as the Boolean condition is true. "While" loops might not run at all if the variable "x" isn't defined. The "while" loop below prints out "Hello" and then increases the value of x by 1. When x reaches 6, it stops printing "Hello."

```
x = 3
while x < 6:
    print "Hello"
    x = x+1
```

Many text languages, such as Python, use **indentation** to show the code that should be included in a loop.

Lists and Tables

Using lists or tables for conditional values can be helpful in languages that allow you to make them. Organizing the conditional values will make the code easier to read and **debug**. It also makes the program run faster on your computer. Programming languages may use "case," "switch," or other terms to signal a list of items to consider. For example, Ruby uses the "case" statement.

The code on page 19 shows a "case" statement in Ruby. The code allows you to **input** a list of ages—such as "0..3," which means ages 0 to 3—and then it outputs the correct school for the age. If the age is greater than 12, the program outputs "school unknown." This code is less work for the computer than multiple "if" statements. That makes the application run faster.

Breaking the Code

Debugging is the process of finding and removing errors that keep a program from working correctly. The process of debugging can be aided by tools in coding programs. These programs will show lines where errors in the code appear.

Here is a code that demonstrates the use of “case” in Ruby.

```ruby

age = 13

grade = case age
  when 0..3 then "no school"
  when 4 then "preschool"
  when 5..10 then "elementary"
  when 10..12 then "middle school"
  else "school unknown"
end
puts grade
```

Your Turn to Try!

Imagine you want to draw a square. First, you need to ask the question: "What is a square?" Then, think of how to make it. You move forward to create a line and then turn left to set up a right angle. This two-step action should repeat four times to create a square. This is similar to creating a simple loop, or a "for" loop in Python. In Python, the code would be:

```
For i in range  (0,3):
    forward(20)
    left(90)
```

Next, try to think about writing a "case" statement. The pseudocode for "case" is expressed in the following statement.

```
CASE expression OF
    Condition 1: sequence 1
    Condition 2: sequence 2
    Default
ENDCASE
```

Imagine that you want to enter the specific name of an animal and have the program tell you if it is a mammal, a bird, an amphibian, or an insect. Using the "case" pseudocode on page 20 and looking back to page 18 if you need help, try to write pseudocode explaining what will happen.

Using a list of animals and their related category is a faster way to have the computer make its choices.

eagle (bird)

crow (bird)

dog (mammal)

frog (amphibian)

cat (mammal)

Conditionals Are Important

Using conditionals in coding allows the coder to have the application make a choice based on the information given. In a simple "if-then" statement, one comparison is being made. One output is possible. If the statement is not true, there is no output. In "if-then-else" statements, one comparison is being made but two outputs are possible. In simple loops, the comparison is made by counting the number of times the loop has run until a specified number is met. In "case" statements, a more **complex** comparison is made with a list.

Conditionals are very important in coding. When conditionals work correctly, you just have to input information and let the program do the work for you!

answer to problem on page 20

```
INPUT animal

CASE Classification expression OF animal
        cat : mammal
        dog: mammal
        frog : amphibian
        eagle : bird
        crow : bird
        default : unknown
ENDCASE

OUTPUT The animal (animal) is in
classification (classification)
```

Glossary

artificial intelligence: An area of computer science that deals with giving machines the ability to seem like they have human intelligence.

clarify: To make something easier to understand.

complex: Having to do with something with many parts that work together.

computer language: A formal language designed to communicate instructions to a machine.

debug: To remove the mistakes from a computer program.

diverge: To split and move out in different directions from a single point.

indentation: The space at the beginning of a written line or paragraph.

input: Information entered into a computer.

logic: The science that studies the formal processes used in thinking and reasoning.

output: Information produced by a computer, or the act of producing that information.

statement: Something you say or write.

time-sharing: Use of a central computer by many users at different locations at the same time.

variable: A quantity that may change when other conditions change.

variation: A change in the form of something.

Index

A
artificial intelligence, 6, 7

B
Boolean, 10, 11, 12, 17

C
code, 6, 10, 12, 16, 17, 18, 19, 20
computer languages, 6, 8, 10, 11, 13, 15, 16, 17, 18

D
debugging, 18

E
elif, 14
"else if" statement, 14, 15
elsif, 14

F
formalism, 6
Frost, Robert, 4

I
"if-then" statement, 4, 8, 10, 11, 12, 22
"if-then-else" statement, 12, 13, 15, 22
input, 18, 22

J
Java, 8

L
lists, 18
logic, 6, 10
loops, 16, 17, 20, 22

M
McCarthy, John, 6, 7

O
output, 13, 14, 18, 22

P
pseudocode, 10, 11, 12, 20, 21
Python, 8, 11, 14, 17, 20

R
recursion, 6
Ruby, 8, 11, 13, 14, 15, 18, 19

T
tables, 18
time-sharing, 6

W
WeDo, 16, 17

Websites

Due to the changing nature of Internet links, PowerKids Press has developed an online list of websites related to the subject of this book. This site is updated regularly. Please use this link to access the list: www.powerkidslinks.com/kcc/cond